I0776390

The Story of a Special Day
Volume 289

October
15

The 288th day of the year (289th in leap years). There are 77 days remaining until the end of the year.

by Michael Dobson

Timespinner
Press

Copyright © and trademarked ™ 2017 by Timespinner Press. All rights reserved, subject to the terms of licenses for photographs and other materials used herein. For a complete list of licenses and accompanying links, see the "Copyright, Credit, and Contact" section toward the end of this book. The Timespinner Press logo is a trademark of Timespinner Press.

This book is also available in e-book form for Kindle, e-pub devices, and other formats from your favorite online booksellers.

For more information about the series, about us, or about your special day, please email us at editor@timespinnerpress.com.

Look for other volumes in *The Story of a Special Day,* coming often. See www.timespinnerpress.com for details and for the most recent information.

Table of Contents

Cover: The Montgolfier brothers launch the first manned flight, October 15, 1783 — the **Cover Story.**

Quote of the Day

"Politics is not the art of the possible. It consists in choosing between the disastrous and the unpalatable."

John Kenneth Gailbraith, economist
in a letter to US President John F. Kennedy
Gailbraith was born October 15, 1908

Today in History

October 15

"October," by Eugène Grasset

What Happened on October 15?

While some days of the year are more famous than others, every day of the year is filled with important, exciting, and unusual events, from religious awakenings to natural disasters, from wars to breakthroughs in technology, and from tragedy to triumph.

In this section, you'll learn about all the events that make October 15 important, including the special event that makes up our cover story or event of the day. Some events you may already know about, others may be new to you, but all of them are important parts of the history of the work.

Let's explore some of the reasons why October 15 is a very special day!

A collectible card of the first test flight by the Montgolfier brothers

Cover Story
First Manned Flight (1783)

The Montgolfier brothers, Joseph-Michel and Jacques-Étienne, invented the first hot air balloon. On October 15, 1783, they tested their balloon for the first time with a human passenger, Étienne, and later on the same day with a different passenger, Pilâtre de Rozier. The balloon was tethered, so the flights only reached a height of 80 feet (24m), the length of the tether. This was the first manned flight in history.

Jacques-Étienne Montgolfier

Joseph-Michel Montgolfier

Joseph-Michel and Jacques-Étienne were born to a wealthy family of paper manufacturers. Joseph-Michel was the twelfth child out of 16. He was known as a maverick and a dreamer.

Jacques-Étienne, the 15th child, was by contrast practical and businesslike, and eventually took over the family business. He and his brother made numerous technical innovations in paper manufacturing, including the first transparent paper and a self-acting hydraulic ram.

Joseph-Michel was the first to become interested in aeronautics. He built parachutes and once jumped from the roof of the family house. One evening, while watching a fire, he noticed the embers flying up from the flames, and wondered how he could harness that force to allow travel in the air.

He built a box-like chamber out of thin wood and covered it with taffeta, and placed it on a stand over a fire. The box lifted off the stand and collided with the ceiling. Excited, he shared his discovery with Jacques-Étienne. They built a larger box and tried a test flight, but the box got away from them and crashed nearly two kilometers away.

After further experiments, the brothers designed a globe-shaped balloon made of sackcloth lined with paper, covered by a fishnet. On June 4, 1783, they flew their balloon in public for the first time, in an unmanned trip that lasted about ten minutes.

The next balloon, named *Aérostat Réveillon*, was significantly larger, 37,500 cubic feet (1060 m^3) in capacity. It was made of taffeta coated with alum, painted blue and decorated with gold designs.

At the time, there was concern about the effects on people flying into the upper atmosphere. Louis XVI suggested sending up a couple of convicted criminals, but the brothers used animals instead.

The sheep (named Montauciel, or "Climb-to-the-sky") was selected because it was a mammal, expected to have a response similar to a human.

The first balloon flight with living beings, September 19, 1783

The duck was chosen as a control, because it was already able to flight at height and would therefore not be affected. The rooster, a bird but one that did not fly, was another control.

The animals all survived, and the king allowed the brothers to test with humans. This time, the brothers built a 60,000 cubic foot (1,700 m^3) balloon, and on October 15, 1783, Jacques-Étienne became the first human to lift off from the Earth.

A little more than a month later, on November 21, 1783, the brothers took their invention public, and demonstrated the first free flight (non-tethered). The crew for that flight consisted of Pilâtre de Rozier and the Marquis d'Arlandes. This flight reached an altitude of 3,000 feet (910m) above Paris, and traveled about nine kilometers in 25 minutes.

While there are various claims to have been the first to fly dating back to the year 559, the Montgolfier flight is the first to be widely accepted. As of October 15, 1783, humans finally "slipped the surly bonds of earth/ and danced the skies on laughter-silvered wings." The age of flight had begun.

A celebration of the Montgolfier brothers

Marie Antoinette, by Élisabeth Vigée Le Brun

Other October 15 Events

From the creation of great works of engineering and art, to devastating wars and natural disasters, thousands of years of history have left their mark on each and every day of the year. Here are some important events that occurred on October 15. (Illustrated items are shaded.)

1582 — In most of Catholic Europe, the **Gregorian calendar**[*] (a major calendar reform initiated by Pope Gregory XIII) goes into effect. The previous day had been October 4, so eleven days in 1582 don't exist.

1793 — During the French Revolution, Queen **Marie Antoinette** of France is tried and convicted of high treason; she is executed the next day.

1815 — Deposed French emperor **Napoleon Bonaparte** arrives on the remote island of Saint Helena to begin his exile. He dies in captivity May 5, 1821, and his body is returned to France in 1840. *(Photo page 16.)*

1888 — The "From Hell" letter, purported to be from **Jack the Ripper**, is received by George Lusk of the Whitechapel Vigilance Committee. The letter includes half a human kidney claimed to have been taken from one of his victims. *(Photo page 17.)*

------

[*] For more on the difference between the Julian "Old Style" calendar and the Gregorian "New Style" calendar, see "What Day of the Week is October 15?"

Napoleon on Saint Helena, by Charles de Steuben

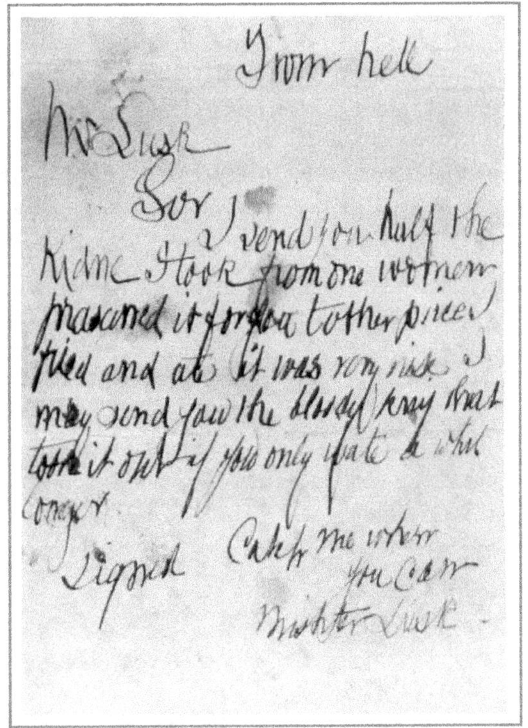

The "From Hell" letter by Jack the Ripper, postmarked October 15, 1888. The text reads as follows (original spelling preserved):

From hell.

Mr Lusk,
Sor
I send you half the Kidne I took from one woman prasarved it for you tother piece I fried and ate it was very nise. I may send you the bloody knif that took it out if you only wate a whil longer

signed

Catch me when you can Mishter Lusk

1894 — French officer Alfred Dreyfus is arrested for giving military secrets to the enemy. He will be convicted and sentenced to Devil's Island in what later turns out to be a major miscarriage of justice. A national scandal, the **Dreyfus Affair**, results.

1923 — In an effort to stop **hyperinflation**, the **German** government introduces a new currency, the *Rentenmark*, which replaces the now-worthless *Papiermark*. The exchange rate was 1 Rentenmark = 1 billion[†] Papiermarks, with a Rentenmark worth roughly US25¢.

A 100 billion Papiermark note, worth 100 Rentenmarks, or around US$25.

---

† The words "billion" and "trillion" have different meanings in depending on where you live. The US and Britain use the "short scale." In that system, a *billion* is 1,000 million (10^9) and a *trillion* is 1,000 billion (10^{12}). A number of other nations, including Germany, use the "long scale," in which 1,000 million (10^9) is a *milliard*, 1 million million (10^{12}) is a *billion*, and 1 million million (10^{18}) is a *trillion*. The "billion" mentioned above is a "long scale" billion, equivalent to a "short scale" trillion.

1928 — The LZ129 *Graf Zeppelin* lands in the US after completing its first transatlantic crossing.

The *Graf Zeppelin* lands at Lakehurst, New Jersey, on October 15, 1928, completing its first transatlantic crossing. (Photo: P&A)

1951 — The pioneering television sitcom *I Love Lucy* premiers. It becomes the most watched show in the US in four of its six seasons. *(Photo page 62.)*

1966 — The **Black Panthers**, a revolutionary black nationalist organization is founded by Bobby Seale and Huey Newton.

1969 — A massive nationwide demonstration, the **Moratorium to End the War in Vietnam**, takes place.

1997 — The **first supersonic land speed record** is set by Andy Green driving ThrustSSC, achieving a speed of 714,144 mph / 1149.303 kph on a mile run. The event takes place 50 years and 1 day following Chuck Yeager's first supersonic flight.

Quote of the Day

"Let us go singing as far as we go: the road will be less tedious."

Virgil, poet
born October 15, 70 BCE

Births
and
Deaths
THERIACA MAGNA
October 15

John L. Sullivan, last world heavyweight bare-knuckle boxing champion and first world heavyweight gloved boxing champion. Sullivan was born October 15, 1858.

Notable October 15 People

With the current world population at about seven billion people, on average about 19 million people also celebrate their birthdays on October 15 — and that isn't counting millions and millions who came before! No matter when you were born, you share your birthday with many special people whose accomplishments (and occasionally embarrassments) have been noted as part of history.

In this section, you'll meet fascinating people who share your birthday. They're organized by what they're famous for, and then in reverse chronological order from most recent to earliest. Those who are shown in photographs or artwork have a box around them. We don't have photos of everyone, so please forgive us if your favorite person is missing.

Some of these people you've heard of, others will be new to you, but they all make up an important part of the reason that October 15 is a truly special day!

Self-portrait, by James Tissot (1865)

Who Was Born on October 15?

Adventure and Heroism

Malcolm Ross, scientist who set an altitude record for manned balloon flight in 1961 that has not at the time of writing been broken. *(1919)*

Varian Fry, American journalist who ran a rescue network in Vichy France that helped thousands of Jewish refugees escape from Nazi hands. *(1907)*

Frederick Fleet, lookout aboard RMS *Titanic* who first sighted the iceberg and notified the bridge. He had not been issued binoculars for his job, and testified that with binoculars, he might have seen it early enough to avoid a collision. *(1887)*

Art

James Tissot, French painter and illustrator known for his portraits of fashionably dressed women. *(1836) (See also page 66.)*

Business and Economics

Emeril Lagasse, restauranteur and celebrity chef known for his television series *Emeril Live*, and his trademark expressions "Kick it up a notch" and "Bam!" *(1959) (Photo page 26)*

  Michael Dobson

Emeril Lagasse (Photo: Denise Gold USAF)

Lee Iacocca, American automobile executive who was president and CEO of Chrysler Corporaion in the 1980s, and who developed the Mustang and Pinto for Ford in the 1960s. *(1924)*

John Kenneth Galbraith, American economist and diplomat who received the Medal of Freedom for his war efforts and the Presidential Medal of Freedom for his contributions to economics. *(1908)*

John Kenneth Galbraith (Courtesy Dutch National Archives/Spaarnestad Photo, CC BY-SA 3.0)

Government and Military

Sarah, Duchess of York, controversial former spouse of the Queen's second son Andrew. *(1959)*

David Trimble, British politician who shared the 1998 Nobel Peace Prize for his work in negotiating the Good Friday Agreement aimed at lessening sectarian violence in Northern Ireland. *(1935)*

Hiram Fong, Hawaiian politician who was the first Asian American and Chinese American elected to be a United States Senator. *(1906)*

Akbar the Great, emperor who expanded the Mughal Empire to encompass nearly all the Indian subcontinent. *(1542)*

Literature and Poetry

Ed McBain, crime fiction writer best known for his novels featuring the 87th Precinct. *(1926)*

Italo Calvino, Italian journalist and author of the *Our Ancestors* trilogy and *Invisible Cities;* received numerous awards, including the French Legion of Honor, the Austrian State Prize for European Literature, and the World Fantasy Life Achievement Award. *(1923)*

Akbar the Great riding an elephant (c. 1609-10)

Mario Puzo, novelist best known for his 1969 novel *The Godfather*; received an Academy Award for Best Adapted Screenplay for his film script. *(1920)*

Arthur Schlesinger Jr., won the Pulitzer Prize for Biography for his 1966 work *A Thousand Days: John F. Kennedy in the White House. (1917)*

C. P. Snow, English author and scientist best known for his novel series *Strangers and Brothers. (1905)*

S. S. Van Dine, author of the popular detective novel series featuring Philo Vance. *(1888)*

P. G. Wodehouse, English author and humorist best known for his stories of such characters as Jeeves and Bertie Wooster, Psmith, and others. *(1881)*

Mikhail Lermontov (Михаи́л Ле́рмонтов), influential Russian novelist and poet known as the "poet of the Caucasus". *(1814‡)*

Virgil, Roman poet best known for writing *The Aeneid,* the national epic of ancient Rome, and for serving as Dante's fictional guide to Hell in *The Divine Comedy. (70 BCE)*

---

‡ Russia converted from the Julian to the Gregorian calendar much later than the rest of Europe. (See "What Day of the Week is October 15?"). Lermontov was born when the Julian calendar was in effect and died under the Gregorian calendar, so his dates of birth and death are usually written showing both dates. He was born October 15 Gregorian, but October 3 "Old Style" Julian.

from "Jeeves in the Springtime" by **P. G. Wodehouse** (Credit: A. Wallis
Mills), *Strand* Magazine, 1921)

The Carpenters. From left, Karen Carpenter, **Richard Carpenter**
(Photo: Robert L. Knudsen, White House staff photographer)

Music

Keyshia Cole, singer-songwriter and television personality who had three platinum albums. *(1981)*

Tito Jackson, member of the Jackson 5 and later a solo artist. *(1953)*

Chris de Burgh, singer-songwriter best known for his 1986 love song "The Lady in Red," which became an international hit. *(1948)*

Richard Carpenter, American pop musician best known as a member of The Carpenters with his sister Karen. *(1946)*

Don Stevenson, drummer and singer-songwriter for the rock band Moby Grape. *(1941)*

Barry McGuire, singer-songwriter best known for his 1965 recording "Eve of Destruction." *(1926)*

Performing Arts

Bailee Madison, child actress in *Bridge to Terabithia, Wizards of Waverly Place,* and *Once Upon a Time.* *(1999)*

Devon Gummersall, actor best known as Brian Krakow on *My So-Called Life.* *(1978)*

Dominic West, actor known for playing Jimmy McNulty in *The Wire* and his award-winning turn as a serial killer in *Appropriate Adult. (1969)*

Todd Solondz, filmmaker known for *Welcome to the Dollhouse. (1959)*

Mira Nair, Indian-American filmmaker known for *Mississippi Masala, Monsoon Wedding,* and *Salaam Bombay! (1957)*

Jere Burns, actor known for his roles on *Dear John, Burn Notice,* and *Justified. (1954)*

Candida Royalle, pornographic actress and filmmaker of couples-oriented pornography. *(1950)*

Haim Saban, producer and distributor of children's television programs, most famously *Mighty Morphin Power Rangers* and its various spinoffs. *(1944)*

Penny Marshall, actress and director initially known for playing Laverne on the sitcom *Laverne & Shirley;* later a director of such films as *Big, Awakenings,* and *A League of Their Own. (1943)*

Linda Lavin, actress best known for playing the title character in the long-running sitcom *Alice. (1937)*

Jean Peters, Hollywood actress and second wife of Howard Hughes whose films included *Pickup on South Street, Captain from Castille, Niagara, Three Coins in the Fountain,* and *Apache. (1926)*

Penny Marshall in *Laverne & Shirley*

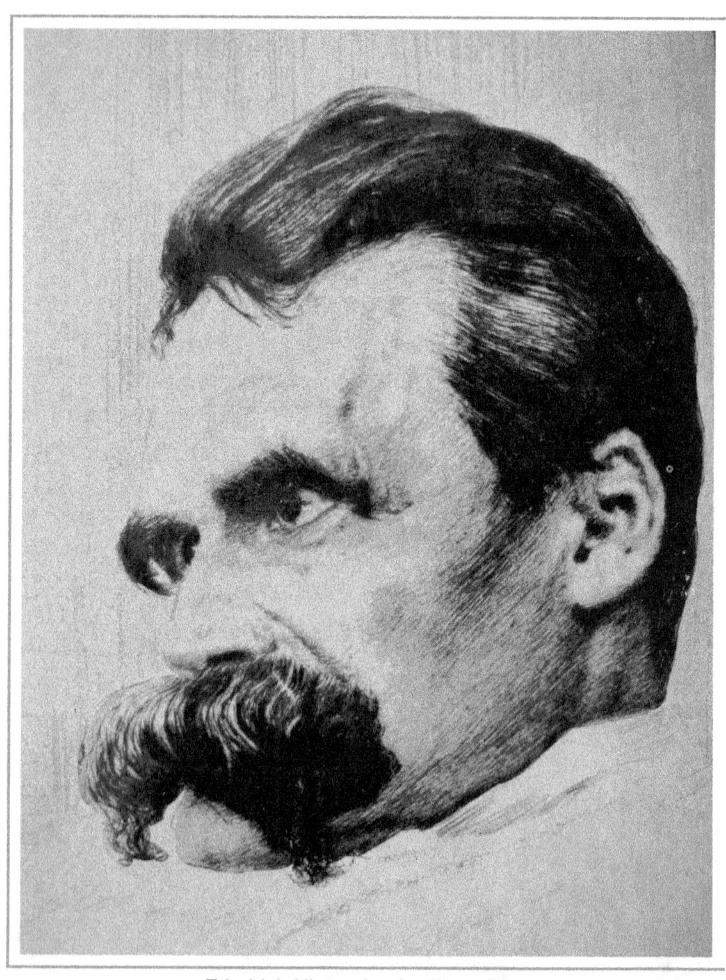

Friedrich Nietzsche, by Hans Olde

Jan Miner, actress best known as Madge the manicurist in a series of television commercials for Palmolive dishwashing detergent ("You're soaking it it") that ran for 27 years. *(1917)*

Mervyn LeRoy, filmmaker whose best known works include *Little Caesar, Million Dollar Mermaid, Mister Roberts,* and *Gypsy. (1900)*

Philosophy and Religion

Friedrich Nietzsche, philosopher, cultural critic, and scholar considered of the most important philosophers of the 19th century. *(1844)*

Lucretius, Roman philosopher and poet known for his writings about Epicurianism. *(99 BCE)*

Science and Technology

Peter Doherty, Australian veterinary surgeon who shared the 1996 Nobel Prize in Physiology or Medicine for his work describing how the body's immune cells protect against viruses. *(1940)*

Asaph Hall, American astronomer best known for his discovery of Deimos and Phobos, the two moons of Mars. *(1829)*

Evangelista Torricelli, Italian physicist and mathematician best known as the inventor of the barometer. *(1608)*

Sports

Jim Palmer, pitcher with the Baltimore Orioles for nineteen years; named to the Baseball Hall of Fame. *(1945)*

Willie O'Ree, first black player in the National Hockey League. *(1935)*

Bobby Morrow, American sprinter who won three gold medals in the 1956 Olympics. *(1935)*

Charley O'Leary, baseball shortstop who was the oldest player to appear in a game, record a hit, and score a run in a career that ran from 1904 to 1934. In the off-season O'Leary was part of a vaudeville act that inspired the 1949 Gene Kelly / Frank Sinatra film *Take Me Out to the Ballgame. (1875)*

John L. Sullivan, legendary boxer who was the last heavyweight champion of bare-knuckle boxing and the first heavyweight champion of gloved boxing. *(1858) (Photo page 22.)*

Jim Palmer (Photo: Keith Allison, CC BY-SA 2.0)

Charley O'Leary baseball card from 1911

Mata Hari, exotic dancer and convicted spy. She died October 15, 1917.
(Photo: P. Boyer, 1905)

Who Died on October 15?

Business

Herbert Henry Dow, founded Dow Chemical Company. *(1930)*

Crime and Punishment

Carlo Gambino, boss of the Gambino crime family and leader of the Mafia governing body The Commission. *(1976)*

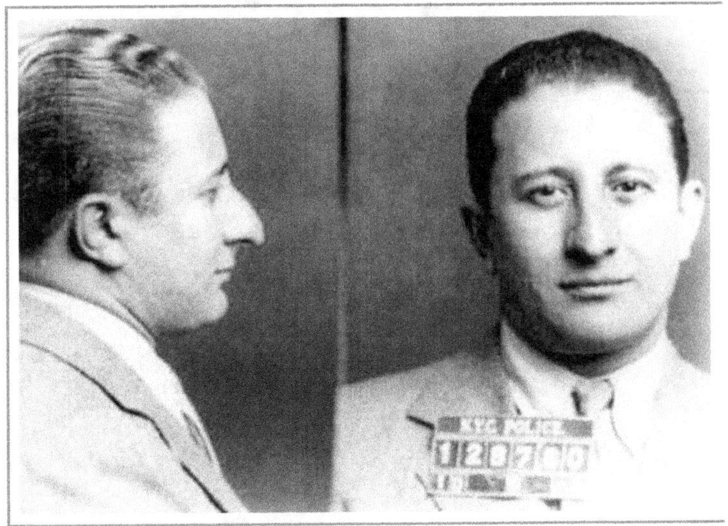

Mug shot of Carlo Gambino (NYPD)

Government

Norodom Sihanouk, King of Cambodia, later Prime Minister following his abdication, and later king again. *(2012) (See also page 51.)*

Norodom Sihanouk in coronation regalia, 1941

Journalism and Literature

Vincent Canby, best known as the chief film critic of *The New York Times. (2000)*

Robert Herrick, lyric poet whose best known work is "To the Virgins, to Make Much of Time," which begins with the famous line, "Gather ye rosebuds while ye may." *(1674)*

Military and Espionage

Hermann Göring, World War I fighter ace and early member of the Nazi party; oversaw the creation of the Gestapo and served as commander-in-chief of the Luftwaffe; convicted at the Nuremberg trials and sentenced to death, but committed suicide the night before his execution. *(1946)*

Hermann Göring
(Photo: Georg Pahl, courtesy Bundesarchiv, CC BY-SA 3.0)

Mata Hari, Dutch exotic dancer convicted and executed as a German spy during World War I. *(1917) (Photo page 40.)*

Tadeusz Kościuszko, Polish-Lithuanian military leader who fought on the US side during the American Revolutionary War and designed the fortifications as West Point; also known as a national hero in Poland, Lithuania, and Belarus *(1817)*

Tadeusz Kościuszko, by Kazimierz Wojniakowski

Music

Cole Porter, Broadway and popular song composer whose many hits include "Night and Day," "Begin the Beguine," and "I Get a Kick Out of You." *(1964)*

Performing Arts

Betty Driver, appeared in more than 2,800 episodes of the British soap opera *Coronation Street. (2011)*

Edie Adams, actress and singer known for her work with television comedian Ernie Kovacs and for her commercials for Muriel cigars. *(2008)*

Edie Adams (left) and Ernie Kovacs in *Take a Good Look*

Pat O'Brien, actor known for such films as *Knute Rockne, All American; Angels With Dirty Faces*; and *Some Like It Hot. (1983)*

Clara Kimball Young, star of the silent film era who didn't survive the transition to talkies. *(1960)*

Science and Medicine

Konrad Emil Bloch, biochemist who shared the 1964 Nobel Prize in Physiology or Medicine for his discoveries related to cholesterol and fatty acid metabolism. *(2000)*

Andreas Vesalius, Flemish physician known as the founder of modern human anatomy. *(1564)*

Sports

Horton Smith, American golfer who won the first and third Masters Tournaments; member of the World Golf Hall of Fame. *(1963)*

Stanley Ketchel, world middleweight boxing champion known as the "Michigan Assassin;" murdered during a robbery at age 24. *(1910)*

Clara Kimball Young on the cover of *Photoplay*, May 1920 issue

Quote of the Day

"To say that his conscience was clear would be inaccurate, for he did not have a conscience, but he had what was much better, an alibi."

P. G. Wodehouse, writer
born October 15, 1881

Holidays
Around
the World

October 15

Washing Hands, by Dante Gabriel Rossetti—for **Global Handwashing Day**

October 15 Events

If you're looking for a reason to take your special day off, you should know that every single day is a holiday somewhere in the world! Here's some of what you can celebrate on October 15!

General Events

Eid El Jala' (Tunisia)

The nation of Tunisia observes Evacuation Day as a public holiday each October 15.

Global Handwashing Day (international)

The importance of handwashing with soap in disease prevention is observed on October 15.

King Father's Commemoration Day (Cambodia)

Cambodia celebrates a national holiday to commemorate its King-Father Norodom Sihanouk. *(Photo page 42.)*

White Cane Safety Day (United States)

The achievements of people who are blind or visually impaired is celebrated in the US each October 15.

Food Days

In the United States, almost every day of the year is dedicated to a particular food. (Some other countries also have official food days, but only in America is there one every single day!) Sponsored by manufacturers, retailers, farmers, or simply fans, these days are often proclaimed by the President, Congress, state governors, or mayors. Given that there are more different foods than days of the year, some days honor more than one kind of food!

In the US, October 15 is **National Mushroom Day.** The average person eats about six pounds (2.7 kg) of mushrooms per year.

Although mushrooms are neither meat nor vegetable, their texture makes them known as the "meat" of the vegetable world. Some mushrooms are hunted in the wild (though care must be taken because some poisonous varieties look like edible ones), but most are cultivated. China produces about half of all cultivated mushrooms worldwide.

Some mushrooms also have medicinal properties, especially in traditional Chinese medicine.

According to some sources, October 15 is also **National Red Wine Day.** Red wines are primarily made from dark-colored grape varieties, but the red color comes from the grape skin rather than the fruit itself. Wines are known to have existed as long as 9,000 years ago, and the oldest known winery is more than 6,100 years old.

Still-Life With Mushrooms, by Ivan Khrutsky (1842)
for **National Mushroom Day**

Monk Testing Wine by Antonio Salvador Casanova y Estorach (1886)
for **National Red Wine Day**

Food Months

The entire month of October is used to celebrate numerous foods. Here's a list of what to eat this month!

- National Apple Month
- National Applejack Month
- National Caramel Month
- National Cookie Month
- National Dessert Month
- National Pasta Month
- National Pickled Peppers Month
- National Pizza Month
- National Popcorn Poppin' Month
- National Pork Month
- National Pretzel Month
- National Seafood Month

Still Life — Study of Apples by William Rickarby Miller
for National Apple Month

Advertising poster of a woman eating almond cookies
for **National Cookie Month**

Religious Feast Days and Holidays

Saint Days

Each day in the year is considered a feast day for one or more saints. They are somewhat different in western Christianity (Catholicism and many forms of Protestantism) and in eastern (Orthodox) Christianity.

In *Western Christianity*, October 15 is the feast day of Saints Bruno of Querfurt, Cúan of Ahascragh, Teresa of Ávila, and Thecla of Kitzingen.

In *Eastern Orthodox Christianity*, it is also the commemoration of Saints Sabinus of Catania, Agileus, Aurelia of Strasbourg, Severus of Trier, Antiochus of Lyon, Cannatus, Fortunatus, Leonard of Vandoeuvre, Odilo, Callistus, Bruno of Merseburg, Willa, John of Suzdal, and Dionysius of Suzdal. (These saints are honored on October 2 by "Old Calendrists[§].")

Non-Gregorian Religious Events

Not every culture uses the familiar Gregorian calendar, so some events may shift days or months over the years. Here is a selection of primarily religious events around the world that sometimes take place on or include October 15.

- Chaturmas (ranges from July 4 to October 31; Hinduism, Jainism)

[§] "Old Calendrists" use the older Julian calendar for liturgical purposes rather than the modern Gregorian one. See "What Day of the Week is October 15?" for the differences between the Julian and Gregorian calendars.

- Dhanteras (September/October, Hinduism)
- Diwali (mid-October to mid-November, Hinduism)
- Lakshmi Puja (September/October, Hinduism)
- Sukkot (late September to late October; Judaism and Samaritanism)

Saint Teresa of Ávila by François Gérard

Honorary Months

Nations around the world issue proclamations recognizing particular months to honor certain causes. If not otherwise specified, all months are US. Here are some honorary designations for October.

Culture

- Black History Month (UK)
- Filipino American History Month
- German American Heritage Month (September 15 — October 15 in the US)
- Hispanic Heritage Month (September 15 — October 15 in the US)
- Italian American Heritage Month
- LGBT History Month
- Polish American Heritage Month

Health

- American Pharmacists Month
- Brain Tumor Awareness Month (Canada)
- Breast Cancer Awareness Month
- Dental Hygiene Month
- Down Syndrome Awareness Month
- Dwarfism/Little People Awareness Month
- Dyslexia Awareness Month
- Eczema Awareness Month
- Health Literacy Month
- Healthy Lung Month
- Infertility Awareness Month

- Liver Awareness Month
- Medical Ultrasound Awareness Month
- Physical Therapy Month
- Spina Bifida Awareness Month
- Sudden Infant Death Syndrome (SIDS) Awareness Month
- World Blindness Awareness Month

The Blind Girl by John Everett Millais
for **World Blindness Awareness Month**

Other

- Bat Appreciation Month
- Black Speculative Fiction Month
- Caffeine Addiction Recovery Month
- Church Library Month
- Class Reunion Month
- Domestic Violence Awareness Month
- Fair Trade Month
- Feral Hog Month
- Financial Planning Month
- International Walk to School Month
- National Adopt a Shelter Dog Month
- National Arts and Humanities Month
- National Cyber Security Awareness Month

Bat Before the Moon, by Biho Takashi — for **Bat Appreciation Month**

Moveable and Multi-Day Events

Some events take place over a specific week or time period. Some events occur on different days each year (such as "fourth Saturday of a month"). These events sometimes take place on or include October 15. All are US unless otherwise specified.

Week-Long Celebrations

- Drink Local Wine Week (2nd full week)
- Earth Science Week (2nd full week)
- Emergency Nurses Week (week that includes October 14)
- Teen Read Week (week including Columbus Day)

Movable Events

- Ada Lovelace Day (mid-October)
- Boss's Day (US, Canada, Lithuania, Romania; work day closest to October 16)
- Emergency Nurses Day (Wednesday of Emergency Nurses Week)
- Teacher's Day (Brazil, 3rd Sunday)
- Mother's Day (Argentina, 3rd Sunday)
- Heroes' Day (Jamaica, 3rd Monday)
- Nanomónestôtse (Native American communities, 3rd Monday)
- International Credit Union Day (3rd Thursday)
- Spirit Day (3rd Thursday)
- Sunday School Teacher Appreciation Day (3rd Sunday)

Just for Fun

Anybody can make up a holiday, and many people do! While none of these are officially recognized and some may come and go, here are a few more holidays for October 15.

- *I Love Lucy* Day (celebrating the 1951 premier of the television series)
- National Grouch Day
- World Toy Camera Day (3rd Sunday)
- Hagfish Day (3rd Wednesday)

The cast of *I Love Lucy* (top) William Frawley, Desi Arnaz (bottom) Vivian Vance, Lucille Ball — for ***I Love Lucy* Day**

October, Hans Thoma

Quote of the Day

"I'm so glad I live in a world where there are Octobers. "

Lucy Maud Montgomery
in *Anne of Green Gables*

About
the
Month
of
October

October, by James Tissot

October: The Tenth Month

The sweet calm sunshine of October, now
Warms the low spot; upon its grassy mould
The purple oak-leaf falls; the birchen bough
Drops its bright spoil like arrow-heads of gold.

— "October," William Cullen Bryant

In Latin, *octo* means eight, so it may seem odd that October is actually the tenth month! The reason goes back to the early Roman calendar, which began the new year in March. What about January and February? They didn't exist, because winter was considered a "monthless" period. Those two months didn't join the calendar until 713 BCE, pushing October from eighth to tenth in the calendar year.

Whether it's the eighth or the tenth month, October has always had 31 days. The last day of October and the last day of February end on the same day of the week in both regular and leap years.

From a seasonal point of view, October is the second month of autumn in the Northern Hemisphere and the second month of spring Down Under. October is the equivalent of April in the other hemisphere.

As an odd bit of trivia, more US presidents have been born in October than any other month: John Adams, Rutherford B. Hayes, Chester A. Arthur, Theodore Roosevelt, and Jimmy Carter.

October in Other Cultures

The month of October has different names in different languages. Some are very similar to English (octobre, oktober, etc.), while some are quite different. Some nations use calendars other than the Gregorian, and their months may overlap with October. In lunar-based calendars, such as the Islamic calendar, months move through the seasons, but many of these languages have a word for October.

Albanian: Tetor

Anglo-Saxon: Wyn-monath (wine month)

Arabic (Egypt, Sudan, Yemen): يونأغينافبرايتشرين الأأكتوبر (uktūbar)

Arabic (Levant): حزيركانوشباتشرين الأول (tishrīn al-awwal)

Arabic (Libya): الصهناالنالتمور، الثمور (at-tumūr; al-tumūr)

Arabic (Morocco, Algeria, and Tunisia): جأيفيفرأكتوبر، أوكتوبر (uktūbər; ūktūbər)

Azerbaijani: Oktyabrl

Basque: Urri

Chinese: 十月 (Cantonese: sahpyuht; Mandarin: shíyuè; Taiwanese: chap-goeh)

Croatian: Listopad

Czech: říjen

Finnish: Lokakuu

Greek: Οκτώβριος (Októbrios)

Haitian Creole: Oktòb

Hebrew: ינפברואוקטובר (ôqtôber)

Hindi: अक्टूबर (aktūbar)

Irish (Gaelic): Deireadh Fómhair mí Dheireadh Fómhair

Italian: Ottobre

Japanese (traditional calendar): 十月 (jūgatsu); 神無月 (kaminaduki)

Khoekhoe (Nama): ǂnûǁnâiseb

Korean: 시월 (siweol)

Lithuanian: Spalis

Manx: Jerrey-fouyir

Maori: Whiringa ā nuku

Old English: Winterfylleþ

Polish: Październik

Quechua: Kantarayki

Russian: октябрь (oktjabr')

Sardinian: Ladàmini

Scottish Gaelic: an t-Sultain

Sesotho: Mphalane

Spanish: Febrero

Swahili: Oktoba

Swazi: iMphala

Thai: Tulakhom

Turkish: Ekim

Ukrainian: жовтень (zhovten)

Vietnamese: 腩迣 (tháng mười)

Welsh: Hydref

Yiddish: פּעברואַאָקטאָבער (oktober)

Zulu: uOkthoba

October Sayings and Superstitions

Here are some sayings and superstitions associated with the month of October.

October Weather Superstitions

Rain in October means wind in December.

When birds and badgers are fat in October, expect a cold winter.

When berries are many in October, beware a hard winter.

If ducks do slide at Hallowtide, at Christmas they will swim; if ducks do swim at Hallowtide, at Christmas they will slide.

There will always be 29 fine days in October.

If the October moon comes without frost, expect no frost till the moon of November.

Halloween Superstitions

If you see bats flying around your house on Halloween, ghosts and spirits are nearby.

If you go to a crossroads at Halloween and listen to the wind, you will learn all the most important things that will befall you during the next twelve months.

Children born on Halloween are said to have the gift of second sight, and can ward off evil spirits.

If you see a spider on Halloween night, it means the spirit of a departed loved one is watching over you.

If you ring bells on Halloween, you will chase away evil spirits.

And if you want to meet a witch, put your clothes on inside out and walk backwards on Halloween night!

October Wedding Superstitions

If in October you do marry, love will come but riches tarry.

The three luckiest months for a wedding are June, October, and December.

An October bride will be pretty, coquettish, loving, but jealous.

Married when leaves in October thin, toil and hardships for you begin.

October Symbols

Birthstones by Culture: Although a variety of birthstones have been associated with each month, the National Association of Jewelers adopted an official list of stones for each birth month. For October, the stones are *opal* and *tourmaline*.

Other stones associated with October include *aquamarine* and *coral*.

Opal (Photo: D. Pulitzer, CC BY-SA 3.0)

Aquamarine (Photo: Decym92)

Tourmaline (Photo: Cowdisley)

Coral (necklace) (Courtesy Tropenmuseum)

Birth Flowers: *Calendula*, also known as *Marigold*, or *Cosmos*. It is associated with warmth, elegance, and devotion, as well as comfort and healing.

Birth Tree: The ancient Druids associated trees with different months of the year. For people born between September 30 and October 27, the birth tree is *ivy*.

A woman surrounded by ivy. (*La Pia de' Tolome*, by Dante Gabriel Rossetti)

Marigolds, by Dante Gabriel Rossetti

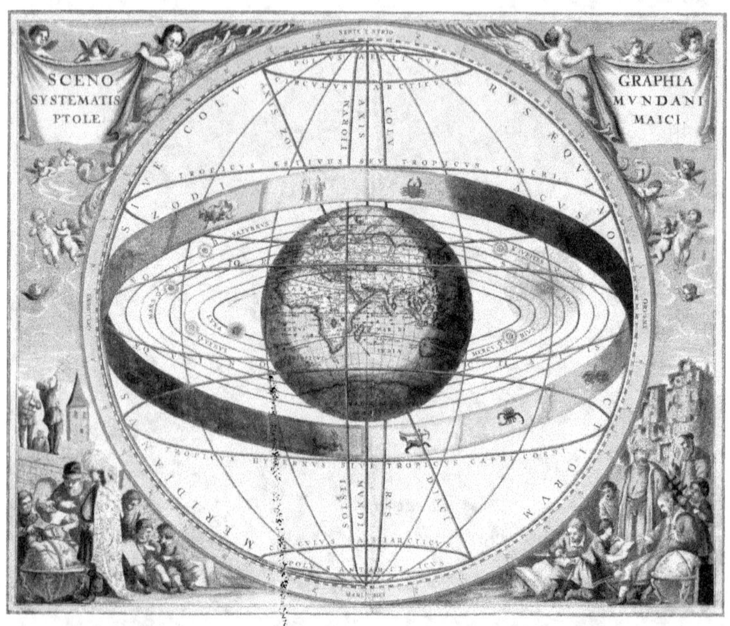

Scenography of the Ptolemaic Cosmography, by Johannes van Loon, based on Andreas Cellarius's *Harmonia Macrocosmica,* 1660

October 15 Zodiac Signs

From the perspective of someone on Earth, the Sun appears to move through the sky throughout the year, along a path astronomers call the *ecliptic plane*. The ecliptic plane is divided into twelve constellations, known as the zodiac, based on traditionally observed patterns of stars. On your birthday, you can't see your constellation, because it's in the daytime sky.

The zodiac was first developed by Babylonian astronomers about 2,500 years ago. Because they were unaware that the Earth wobbles like a spinning top (known as *precession*), they didn't make allowance for the fact that the Sun's path through the zodiac changes over time.

That means there are now two sets of dates for your birth sign. The *tropical dates* are the original Babylonian dates; the *sidereal dates* tell you where the Sun actually appears as it moves along its annual path.

For October 15, the tropical sign is **Libra** and the sidereal sign is **Virgo.**

Libra

Tropical September 23 to October 23
Sidereal October 16 to November 15

The Babylonians considered Libra, the Scales, to be sacred to the sun god Shamash, patron of truth and justice. The Romans reassigned the scales to Astraea, the celestial virgin, better known as Virgo.

Libra is symbolized by the gryphon, a mythological creature with the head, wings, and claws of an eagle and the hind legs of a lion. The Romans believed Libra was the sign "in which the seasons are balanced," and thus idolized this constellation.

Libra is an air sign, and people born under this sign are supposed to be extroverts, socially graceful, and just. Librans are supposed to be compatible with the other air signs of Gemini and Aquarius.

Virgo

Tropical August 23 to September 23
Sidereal September 16 to October 15

The constellation of Virgo was originally associated with the grain harvest and symbolized fertility. The Greeks and Romans saw Virgo as Demeter or Ceres, the goddess of agriculture. In art, Virgo is often represented as carrying two sheaves of wheat. In the Middle Ages, Virgo was also sometimes connected to the Virgin Mary.

In astrology, Virgos are associated with being observant, helpful, and reliable, but can be perceived as inflexible and cold. They are supposed to be compatible with Taurus, Cancer, and Capricorn, but not with Gemini, Libra, or Aries.

Illustration by Edward Penfield

What Day of the Week is October 15?

On what day of the week does October 15 fall?

Surprisingly, this isn't an easy question. Because the calendar year is 365 days long (366 in leap years), it doesn't divide evenly by the seven days of the week.

Also, the Earth goes around the Sun in about 365-1/4 days, so a calendar tends to drift over time. That's why the same date falls on different weekdays in different years.

This is made even more complicated by a change in calendars that took place in 1582. Our modern calendar has its roots in ancient Rome, in a calendar reform conducted by Julius Caesar. Caesar commissioned mathematicians to attack the problem, and they came up with the idea of leap years, and thus standardized the calendar for centuries to come. This was called the Julian calendar.

Over time, however, the small errors in Caesar's calculation compounded. That's why Pope Gregory XIII commissioned the Gregorian calendar, used in most of the world today. Some countries converted in 1582, when the calendar was first developed; some converted later; other still haven't changed.

Gregorian and Julian aren't the only types of calendars. The Hebrew year, the Islamic year, and many other calendars are used in different parts of the world and among different people.

You can convert Gregorian dates to other calendars, including the Hebrew calendar, the Islamic calendar, and even the Mayan calendar by visiting the Fourmilab Calendar Converter at http://www.fourmilab.ch/documents/calendar/.

Chinese calendar systems are quite complex and have changed several times; a full discussion is far beyond the scope of this book. If you're interested, you can find information here: http://www.hermetic.ch/cal_stud/chinese_cal.htm.

On Names and Dates

Historians use "CE" (Common Era) and "BCE" (Before the Common Era) instead of the more common "AD" (Anno Domini, or Year of Our Lord) and "BC" (Before Christ), reflecting the fact that the year-numbering system established by the Gregorian calendar is used throughout the world in many countries not culturally Christian.

The CE/BCE designation dates back to at least 1708, and has been adopted as a standard by the United Nations and the Universal Postal Union. Because this series of books covers events and people of all nations and cultures, we use the CE/BCE terms.

The abbreviation "O.S." ("Old Style") and "N.S." ("New Style") on some dates refers to the fact that the Russian Empire (in particular) did not switch from the Julian to the Gregorian calendar at the same time as the rest of Europe, and therefore some figures and events have two dates.

Also, in the Julian calendar in England in the 16th century, the year began on March 25 rather than January 1. To avoid confusion with Gregorian dates, dates between January and March were often written using both years.

People and events whose original names are not in the Western alphabet have their native names (where possible) in the appropriate script shown in parenthesis. If you are using an e-reader to access an electronic version of this book, all characters don't always display on all devices.

A 50-year brass perpetual calendar.

Quote of the Day

"Time is an illusion, lunchtime doubly so."

Douglas Adams,
from *The Hitchhiker's Guide to the Galaxy*

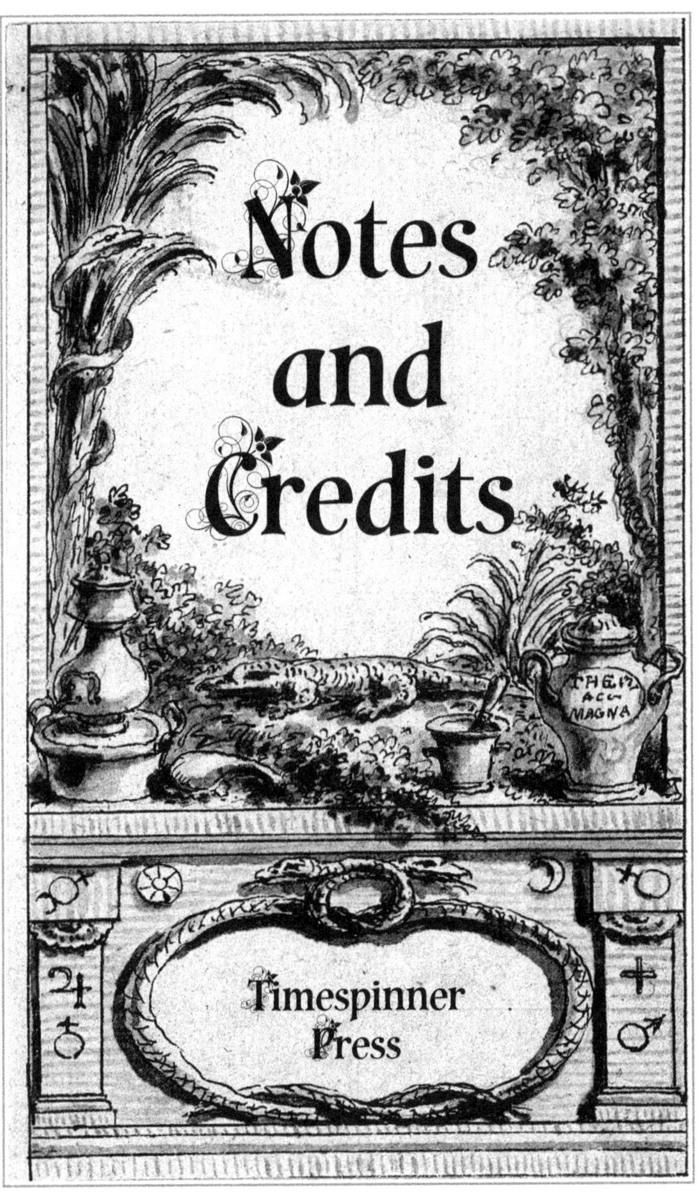
Notes
and
Credits
Timespinner
Press

Cartoon by John T. McCutcheon

Copyright, Credit, and Contact

Follow Us

Our blog "This Day in History" (http://timespinnerpress.com/ this-day-in-history/) features short articles on events and people associated with each day, and updates several times each week. Also subscribe to the "Quote of the Day" at http:// timespinnerpress.com/quote-of-the-day/. You can get daily links by following us on Facebook at TimespinnerPress, or on Twitter as @sidewisethinker.

Contact Us

Find an error or a format problem? Want information about the series, about us, or about when the volume for your special day might be available? Please email us at editor@timespinnerpress.com. (We also take requests if your special day isn't yet complete. Please give us at least six weeks' notice if possible.)

Sources

We owe a great debt to Wikipedia, which is our first stop for research. We attempt to make independent confirmation of all important dates and facts through a variety of other sources.

Other sources we frequently use include the Library of Congress; "on this day" listings from *Encyclopedia Britannica*, the *New York Times*, and the BBC; Omniglot for the names of months in other languages; *Chase's Calendar of Events*; and, of course, the always essential Google.

All art and photographs are either in the public domain, used under a Creative Commons license, or with a "fair use" justification, and most frequently come from Wikimedia Commons and the Library of Congress Prints and Photographs Division.

Attribution is provided where possible, or as requested by the copyright owner, or when there is particular historical significance, listed below. For information about any particular illustration or photograph, please contact us.

Credits

1. The 1783 cover illustration of of the first manned flight of the Montgolfier brothers balloon by Claude-Louis Desrais is in the public domain because its copyright has expired. It is from the collection of the Bildarchiv Preussischer Kulturbesitz, Berlin.

2. The illustration of the month of October used on the back cover is from the French Gothic illuminated manuscript *Les Très Riches Heures du duc de Berry* by the Limbourg Brothers, Jean Colombe, and an intermediate painter whose name is lost to history. It is in the public domain because its copyright has expired.

3. The box graphic used on the first page is from a 1916 pamphlet entitled "Divorce versus Democracy" authored by G. K. Chesterton, originally published in London by the Society of St. Peter and St. Paul. It is in the public domain in the US because it was published prior to 1923, and is in the public domain in all countries (including the country of origin) in which the copyright time is the author's life plus 70 years or less.

4. The graphic design for the section pages in this book is from a design originally created for a pharmacy label. It is courtesy of Wellcome Images (ICV No 11073, photo V0010813), and is used here under CC BY-SA 4.0.

5. The 1896 drawing "October" by Eugène Grasset is in the public domain because its copyright has expired.

6. The first test flight with an aerostat illustration is from a set of collecting cards with pictures of events in ballooning and parachuting history, published between 1890 and 1900 by Romanet & cie., Paris. It is in the public domain because its copyright has expired. It is from the collection of the Library of Congress Prints and Photographs Division, digital ID ppmsca.02562.

7. The 18th century illustration of the first balloon flight carrying living beings is in the public domain because its copyright has expired.

8. The 18th century portrait of Jacques-Étienne Montgolfier is in the public domain because its copyright has expired.

9. The portrait of Joseph-Michel Montgolfier first appeared in the 1887 book *Histoire des ballons et des aéronautes célèbres* by Gaston Tissandier (Paris: H. Launette & Cie.). It is in the public domain because its copyright has expired.

10. The 1783 illustration of the first manned hot-air balloon is by Claude-Louis Desrais, and is in the public domain because its copyright has expired.

11. The illustration celebrating the Montgolfier brothers is from a set of collecting cards with pictures of events in ballooning and parachuting history, published between 1890 and 1900 by Romanet & cie., Paris. It is in the public domain because its copyright has expired. It is from the collection of the Library of Congress Prints and Photographs Division, digital ID ppmsca.02562.

12. The 1783 painting of Marie Antoinette by Élisabeth Vigée Le Brun is in the public domain because its copyright has expired. It is from the collection of the Prince Ludwig von Hessen und bei Rhein, Wolfsgarten Castle, Germany.

13. The 1828 portrait *Napoleon on Saint Helena* by Charles de Steuben is in the public domain because its copyright has expired.

14. The 1888 "From Hell" letter is in the public domain because its copyright has expired.

15. The image of a 100 billion German Papiermark from 1924 is in the public domain under § 5 Abs.1 UrhG as an official work issued by a German federal or state authority, or by a predecessor state.

16. The 1928 photograph of the *Graf Zeppelin* landing at Lakehurst, New Jersey, is by Pacific and Atlantic Photos, and is in the public domain because because it was first published in the United States between 1923 and 1977 without a copyright notice.

17. The photograph of John L. Sullivan by Richard K. Fox originally appeared in *Supplement to Police Gazette*, vol. LXXII, no. 1078, Saturday, April 23, 1898, and is courtesy Library of Congress Prints and Photographs Division, digital ID cph.3c18653. It is in the public domain because its copyright has expired,

18. The 1865 self-portrait of James Tissot is in the public domain because its copyright has expired. It is in the collection of the Fine Arts Museums of San Francisco, Palace of the Legion of Honor.

19. The 2003 photograph of Emeril Lagasse was taken for the US Air Force by Denise Gold, and is in the public domain as a work created by an employee of the US government as part of that person's official duties. The image has been cropped.

20. The 1982 photograph of John Kenneth Galbraith is courtesy of the Dutch National Archives (Nationaal Archief) and Spaarnestad Photo, and is used here under CC BY-SA 3.0 Netherlands.

21. The miniature of Akbar the Great was created around 1609-1610, and is in the public domain because its copyright has expired. It is from the Museen für islamische Kunst, Staatliche Museen zu Berlin.

22. The 1972 photograph of Richard Nixon meeting with The Carpenters was taken by White House staff photographer Robert L. Knudsen, and is in the pubic domain as a work created by an employee of the US government as part of that person's official duties. The image has been cropped.

23. The 1976 publicity photo of Penny Marshall in *Laverne & Shirley* is in the public domain because it was first published in the United States between 1923 and 1977 without a copyright notice. Traditionally, publicity photographs are not copyrighted because of the way in which they are intended to be used.

24. The 1899 portrait of Friedrich Nietzsche by Hans Olde first appeared in *Pan*, Vol. 5, No. 4, pg. 233. It is in the public domain because its copyright has expired.

25. The 2017 photograph of Jim Palmer is copyright © Keith Allison, and is used here under CC BY-SA 2.0. It has been cropped.

26. The 1911 American Tobacco Company trading card of Charley O'Leary is in the public domain because its copyright has expired. It is in the collection of the Library of Congress Prints and Photographs Division, Benjamin K. Edwards Baseball Cards collection, digital ID bbc.1491f.

27. The 1905 photograph of Mata Hari by P. Boyer is in the public domain because its copyright has expired.

28. The 1930s mug shot of Carlo Gambino is in the public domain because it was first published in the United States between 1923 and 1977 without a copyright notice, and because it is a work created by a government employee as part of that person's official duties.

29. The 1941 portrait of Norodom Sihanouk is in the public domain in Cambodia, its country of origin, and in France, who controlled Cambodia in 1941, because its copyright has expired in both nations.

30. The 1932 portrait photograph of Hermann Göring by Georg Pahl is courtesy Deutsches Bundesarchiv (German Federal Archives), Bild 102-13805. It is used here under CC BY-SA 3.0 Germany.

31. The portrait of Tadeusz Kościuszko by Kazimierz Wojniakowski was created prior to 1812 and is in the public domain because its copyright has expired.

32. The 1960 publicity photo from *Take a Good Look* is in the public domain because it was first published in the United States between 1923 and 1977 without a copyright notice.

33.   The cover of the May 1920 issue of *Photoplay* is in the public domain
      because it was first published in the United States prior to January
      1, 1923.
34.   The 1865 painting *Washing Hands* by Dante Gabriel Rossetti is in the
      public domain because its copyright has expired.
35.   The 1842 painting *Naturmort z hrybami* by Ivan Khrutsky is in the
      public domain because its copyright has expired.
36.   The 1886 painting *Monk Testing Wine* by Antonio Salvador Casanova
      y Estorach is in the public domain because its copyright has expired.
      It is in the Brooklyn Museum, accession number 06.336.1.
37.   The 1862 painting *Still Life — Study of Apples by* William Rickarby
      Miller is in the public domain because its copyright has expired. It is
      in the De Young Museum.
38.   The 1900 advertisement for almond cookies by H. Lalo is in the
      public domain because its copyright has expired. It is from the
      Library of Congress Prints and Photographs Division, digital ID
      cph.3g11920.
39.   The detail from the 1827 painting of Teresa of Ávila by François
      Gérard is in the public domain because its copyright has expired. It
      is in the collection of the Infirmerie Marie-Thérèse, Paris.
40.   The 1856 painting *The Blind Girl* by John Everett Millais is in the
      public domain because its copyright has expired. It is in the
      collection of the Birmingham Museum and Art Gallery, United
      Kingdom.
41.   The 1910 woodblock print *Bat Before the Moon* by Biho Takashi is in
      the public domain because its copyright has expired. It is in the
      collection of the Brooklyn Museum.
42.   The publicity photograph from *I Love Lucy* is in the public domain
      because it was first published in the United States between 1923 and
      1977 without a copyright notice.
43.   The illustration "October" by Hans Thoma is from his late 19th
      century book *Festkalendar*. It is in the public domain because its
      copyright has expired.
44.   The 1887 painting *October* by James Tissot is in the public domain
      because its copyright has expired. It is in the collection of the
      Montreal Museum of Arts.
45.   The 1815 woodcut of a proposal is in the public domain because its
      copyright has expired.
46.   The 2013 photograph of a Coober Pedy opal is copyright © D.
      Pulitzer, and is used here under CC BY-SA 3.0.

47. The 2011 photograph of a Cut Kiboko Gold tourmaline is copyright © Cowdisley, and is used here under CC BY-SA 3.0.

48. The 2009 photograph of an aquamarine was released into the public domain by its creator, Decym92.

49. The photograph of a coral necklace was provided to Wikimedia Commons by the National Museum of World Cultures, Tropenmuseum Collection, and is used here under CC BY-SA 3.0.

50. The painting *La Pia de' Tolomei* by Dante Gabriel Rossetti was painted between 1868 and 1880, and is in the public domain because its copyright has expired. It is in the Helen Foresman Spencer Museum of Art, Lawrence, Kansas.

51. The 1873 painting *Marigolds* by Dante Gabriel Rossetti is in the public domain because its copyright has expired. It is in the collection of the Castle Museum and Art Gallery, Nottingham.

52. The celestial sphere is from *Scenography of the Ptolemaic Cosmography*, by Johannes van Loon, based on Andreas Cellarius's *Harmonia Macrocosmica*, 1660. It is in the public domain because its copyright has expired.

53. The 1906 automobile calendar is by Edward Penfield, and is in the collection of the Library of Congress Prints and Photographs Division. It is in the public domain because its copyright has expired.

54. The 50-year perpetual calendar photograph is in the public domain.

55. The cartoon by John T. McCutcheon is from his 1905 collection *The Mysterious Stranger and Other Cartoons by John T. McCutcheon*. It is in the public domain because its copyright has expired.

56. The painting "October," from *Labors of the Month* by Simon Bening, was originally published in the first half of the 16th century, and is in the public domain because its copyright has expired.

57. The painting "October" is from the *Brevarium Grimani*, by Simon Bening, created circa 1510. It is in the public domain because its copyright has expired.

License Description and Terms

Aside from material purely in the public domain, photographs and other material in this book are used under specific licenses permitting free use, usually with an attribution requirement. For full text and terms of these licenses, click or enter the appropriate links below. If you believe there is an error in the copyright status or attribution of any of these images, please email us.

- Creative Commons Attribution 2.0 Generic (CC-BY 2.0): http://creativecommons.org/licenses/by/2.0/deed.en
- Creative Commons Attribution-Share Alike 3.0 Generic (CC-BY-SA 3.0): http://creativecommons.org/licenses/by-sa/3.0/
- Creative Commons Attribution-Share Alike 2.5 Generic (CC-BY-SA 2.5): http://creativecommons.org/licenses/by-sa/2.5/deed.en
- Creative Commons Attribution-Share Alike 2.0 Generic (CC-BY-SA 2.0): http://creativecommons.org/licenses/by/2.0/deed.en
- Creative Commons Attribution-Share Alike 1.0 Generic (CC-BY-SA 1.0): http://creativecommons.org/licenses/by-sa/1.0/deed.en
- CC0 1.0 Universal (CC0 1.0) Public Domain Dedication (CC0 1.0) http://creativecommons.org/publicdomain/zero/1.0/deed.en
- GNU Free Documentation License (GFDL): http://en.wikipedia.org/wiki/Wikipedia:Text_of_the_GNU_Free_Documentation_License
- License Art Libre (Free Art License): http://artlibre.org

Labors of the Months: October, by Simon Bening

Other Books from Timespinner Press

Timespinner
Press

The Story of a Special Day

Michael Dobson

A series of (eventually) 366 volumes covering everything that happened on your special day! Events, births, deaths, quotes, holidays, and much more. It's like a birthday card they'll never throw away!

US$7.95 print / US$2.99 ebook.

From Plassey to Pakistan

Humayun Mirza

The history of British Colonial India and the formation of Pakistan from the unique perspective of the son of Pakistan's first president and last of the royal line of Bengal, Bihar, and Orissa! This unique historical document tells the inside story of this distinguished family, including the detailed story of the coup that toppled his father from power!

US$27.95 print

A Whole New Navy: America's War in the Pacific

Miles Durr

The most comprehensive and detailed description of America's naval war in the Pacific ever—every battle, every ship, every task force and every task group from Pearl Harbor through the Japanese surrender! A must-have for the collection of every World War II buff!

US$29.95 print

Improbable History: The Weird, the Obscure, and the Strangely Important

edited by Michael Dobson

From the birth of Western civilization to the rescue of Apollo 13, from the Leaning Tower of Pisa to Florence's Duomo, history has often turned on small, improbable details. Whatever happened to the ancient Samaritan people? Why did a fortuitous rainstorm allow the British to conquer India? How did an air raid in Italy lead to the development of chemotherapy? What happened when Albert Einstein met Adolf Hitler on the streets of Berlin? How did the Japanese manage to attack the US mainland using balloons? A cast of award-winning writers tackle some of the strangest tales in history!

US$19.95 print

The Letters of William Philip Schwartz 1842-1855

edited by John F. Schwartz

The 19th century soldier and adventurer William Philip Schwartz wrote a series of vivid and detailed letters chronicling his adventures in the Indian Wars, the Mexican-American War, the Gold Rush, and his term as Marine sergeant aboard the USS Constellation. A pioneer in photography, he took *the first known war photographs*. An unforgettable first-hand look into life in the 19th century!

US$17.95 print

Watergate Considered as an Organization Chart of Semi-Precious Stones (and other essays)

by Michael Dobson

In this light-hearted yet insightful tour through the Nixon White House, the Committee to Re-Elect the President, and the various investigative committees, you'll meet fascinating characters from Richard Nixon himself to such lieutenants as a G. Gordon Liddy and John Dean. You'll gain insights into the origin of the scandal, the motives of the players, and how the situation spiraled so badly out of control.

US$9.95 print/US$3.99 ebook

WWW.TIMESPINNERPRESS.COM

 Michael Dobson

"October" from the *Brevarium Grimani* by Simon Bening (c.1510)

www.ingramcontent.com/pod-product-compliance
Lightning Source LLC
Chambersburg PA
CBHW060747260726
48660CB00002B/510